Saigas

Victoria Blakemore

© 2019 Victoria Blakemore

All rights reserved. This book or parts thereof may not be reproduced in any form, stored in any retrieval system, or transmitted in any form by any means—electronic, mechanical, photocopy, recording, or otherwise—without prior written permission of the publisher, except as provided by United States of America copyright law. For permission requests, write to the publisher, at "Attention: Permissions Coordinator," at the address below.

vblakemore.author@gmail.com

Copyright info/picture credits

Cover, Victor Tyakht/Shutterstock; Page 3, Victor Tyakht/Shutterstock; Page 5, dnkkolyan/AdobeStock; Page 7, vzmaze/Shutterstock; Page 9, Maxim Petrichuk/Adobestock; Pages 10-11, Dmitry/AdobeStock; Page 13, Victor Tyakht/Shutterstock; Page 15, dnkkolyan/AdobeStock; Page 17, dnkkolyan/AdobeStock; Page 19, dnkkolyan/AdobeStock; Page 21, Nikolai Denisov/Shutterstock; Page 23; dnkkolyan/AdobeStock; Page 25, Yakov Oskanov/Shutterstock; Page 27, Nikolai Denisov/Shutterstock; Page 29, vzmaze/AdobeStock; Page 31, Victor Tyakht/AdobeStock; Page 33, Victor Tyakht/Shutterstock

Table of Contents

What are Saigas?   2

Size   4

Physical Characteristics   6

Habitat   8

Range   10

Diet   12

Communication   16

Movement   18

Saiga Calves   20

Saiga Life   22

Winter   24

Population   26

Saigas in Danger   28

Helping Saigas   30

Glossary   34

What Are Saigas?

Saigas are large mammals. They are members of the Bovidae family. Other animals in the Bovidae family include impalas, sheep, and bison.

Saigas are a kind of antelope. Like many other antelopes, saigas have a hoof that is split into an even number of toes.

Saigas are usually cream, white, tan, beige, and orange-brown in color.

Size

Saigas usually grow to be between three and five feet long. They stand up to about two and a half feet tall at the shoulder.

When fully grown, saigas can weigh between twenty-five and 110 pounds.

Female saigas are usually much smaller than male saigas.

Physical Characteristics

Saigas are known for their long, oddly shaped nose. It is thought to help saigas warm up the air they breathe in the winter. It can also help to filter out the dust breathed in during the summer.

Saigas have a thick, heavy coat of fur. It is longer and thicker from their head to their chest.

Male saigas have long antlers with sharp points. They use them if they fight with other male saigas.

Habitat

Saigas are found in **semideserts** and **steppes**. Both of these habitats provide saigas with grass to eat, but not many other plants.

Saigas prefer these open areas because it allows them to watch for predators.

Range

Saigas are found in parts of Asia and Europe.

They are found in Russia, Kazakhstan, Uzbekistan, China, and Mongolia.

Diet

Saigas are **herbivores**. They eat only plants.

Their diet is made up of plants such as grass, herbs, shrubs, and lichen. The plants can be tough to **digest**. Saigas get a lot of the water they need from the plants they eat.

Saigas visit watering holes. It is thought that they go there to drink twice each day.

Saigas have a special kind of stomach. Their stomach has four **chambers**.

After they eat, they bring their food, or **cud**, back up and chew on it again. This helps their stomach to **digest** tough plants that many other animals could not eat.

Saigas are most active during the day. They spend their time **grazing** or traveling with their herd.

Communication

Saigas use sound, movement, and scent to communicate. They have been seen signaling other saigas with tail movements.

Male saigas use their scent to mark their territory. The smell tells other male saigas to stay away. They also make a loud roar with their nose to warn other males.

Female saigas have a special trumpeting sound they make when their calves are first born.

Movement

Saigas are able to run at speeds of about fifty miles per hour for short distances. This helps them to quickly escape if there is a predator nearby.

They are often seen swimming to cross rivers. They can also jump into the water to stay safe from a predator.

Saigas usually stay away from areas that are steep. It can be hard for them to see predators or escape there.

Saiga Calves

Saigas have one or two calves in the spring. Many females come together and have their calves at the same time.

Saiga calves are able to start **grazing** a few days after being born. Their mother also feeds them milk for about four months.

Calves are able to run within a day of being born. This helps them to stay safe from predators.

Saiga Life

Saigas are known for their long **migrations** to warmer areas in the winter. They travel in groups called herds. These herds often travel over fifty miles in a day.

Saigas are very **timid** animals. They are quick to run if there is danger nearby, even if they are in a large herd.

Saigas are rarely seen alone. They are almost always seen with their herd.

Winter

Saiga habitats get very cold in the winter. They have a special **adaptation** that helps them to survive.

When it starts to get cold, saigas start to grow a thicker coat of fur. It can be twice as thick as their normal coat. Their thicker fur helps them to stay warm.

The color of a saiga's coat changes in the winter. It becomes a sandy cream color.

Population

Saigas are **critically endangered**. There are very few left in the wild.

Saiga populations have been **declining** in all three areas they are found. If they continue to decline, they could soon become **extinct**.

In the wild, saigas can live between ten and twelve years. Many do not survive that long.

Saigas in Danger

Saigas are facing several threats.

One threat is habitat loss. Saiga habitats are being cleared for **agriculture,** buildings, and roads.

The main threat is that saigas are being hunted by humans. Saigas are hunted for their horns, meat, and bones. Their horns are used in some Asian medicines.

Saigas are **vulnerable** to disease, especially right after they have calves. Some diseases are spread by **livestock** in saiga habitats.

Helping Saigas

Some saigas live in special protected areas. These areas provide animals such as saigas with a safe habitat to live in.

There are laws that try to protect saigas from being hunted. Some laws also prevent saiga horns from being brought into different countries.

Some wildlife centers release saigas that are born there into the wild. This can help the population to grow.

Some groups focus on education. They teach people about saigas and the problems they face. They hope this will make people want to help saigas.

Glossary

Adaptation: a feature that helps an animal survive

Agriculture: farming, raising animals and crops

Chamber: compartment or room

Critically Endangered: an animal that is nearly extinct

Cud: food that animals bring up from their stomach to chew again

Declining: getting smaller

Digest: to break down food into materials that can be used and absorbed by the body

Extinct: when there are no more of an animal left in the wild

Grazing: eating grass

Herbivore: an animal that eats only plants

Livestock: animals such as cows, sheep, and pigs that are kept on farms

Migration: when animals move from one place to another each year, usually due to temperature or food availability

Semidesert: an area that is similar to a desert, but has more grasses and plants

Steppe: a flat area of grassland

Territory: an area of land an animal claims as its own

Timid: shy, fearful of danger

Vulnerable: able to be hurt or injured

About the Author

Victoria Blakemore is a first grade teacher in Southwest Florida with a passion for reading.

You can visit her at

www.elementaryexplorers.com

Also in This Series

Also in This Series

www.ingramcontent.com/pod-product-compliance
Lightning Source LLC
Chambersburg PA
CBHW040221040426
42333CB00049B/3194